Test Automation in the Real World

Practical Lessons for Automated Testing

By Greg Paskal

To all the automation engineers
striving to bring excellence
to our craft…

Table of Contents

Introduction 1
Testing Organizations and Test Automation 5
First Steps into Test Automation 19
Removing The Word Test From Test Automation 25
As Designed vs. As Discovered 31
The Automation Evaluation 35
Art and Soul of a Function Library 45
How to Hire an Automation Engineer 55
ROI Robbers in Test Automation 63
Glossary of Terms 85
Acknowledgments 93

Introduction

"Young man" came the words from my manager, "I want to send you to training and help us learn to build some automated testing." Those words led me on my first business trip from the Aerospace Company located in Southern California to the far off world of Austin, Texas. The weeklong class introduced me to a graphical programming language where I used some of the best computers available in the mid 1980's. We developed our automated tests by connecting icons together, each representing test equipment back in our labs in California.

My usage of automation now spans over 30 years from those first projects at the Aerospace Company. I now work with systems and environments we would never have dreamed of in those early days. It didn't hurt to grow up in a time when computers were just starting to become something a person could own. How grateful I am that my parents bought me a Commodore Vic 20 when I was nineteen years old. I used that computer to learn how to program in BASIC and build circuits that could enhance that computer's capability. Learning about computers, programming and electronics at that time laid an amazing foundation to build upon and I believe gave me many advantages in moving forward in the work I do these days.

Early Days of Test Automation: Thinking back to those early days, our objective was to repeatedly and reliably interact with the test environment to determine its reliability over an extended period of time. Those first automated tests built for the Aerospace Company were designed to "Life Test" devices known as Traveling Wave Tube Amplifiers. These devices would be launched into outer space on a rocket, 22,000 miles above the earth to a place called Geo Synchronous Orbit. My automated "Life Test" would help my team understand how these devices would operate over their lifespan. It was fascinating work and an incredible opportunity to utilize my skills with some amazing technology.

Reacquainted with Test Automation: In 2001 I was offered an amazing job with a company in Ventura, California. The hiring manager knew my passion for technology and my experience as a programmer and brought these together into a position within their QA organization. I was given a box of software and told to install and experiment with it a bit and see if I could figure out how to use it for our testing purposes. After going through the tutorials and learning about the project, I soon had a basic, automated program that would select over ten thousand product variations pertaining to online orders. The team was thrilled; they were now able to see the results of selecting endless possible configurations. We continued to leverage that first test automation effort for many releases; it was simple but effective and I learned the value of developing something quick that could remove tedious work from our team and free them up for other work.

I'm excited to share with you the many lessons I've learned on this journey as an automation engineer. Much of this knowledge was learned in the trenches of countless QA projects. These lessons should be applicable across a wide variety of automation tools and help you to make the most of your automation development endeavors.

Let your journey begin!

Testing Organizations and Test Automation

As companies continue to look for ways to keep cost down, new and emerging technologies surface with promises of saving time and expense. Test Automation falls into one of these technologies with all the promise of timesaving and ease of use. The very idea of automating things has a mystique that enamors even a seasoned technologist and why not, many companies sell variations of tools that can perform the work of a human, automatically with very little up front effort. Herein lies the elusive world of test automation. This chapter provides a real world look at test automation and how to leverage it effectively within your organization.

Recognizing an Opportunity: Test Automation nearly always surfaces within a company when it's realized that a significant amount of testing needs to be done but there is little to no budget to hire more test engineers. Show up to any technology conference and you'll likely encounter a number of vendors promising a simple "Click-and-Record" approach to creating automated test scripts that will run until the end of time with minimal to no effort. It's hard to deny these results when watching one of these "Automated Testing" demonstrations as the sample script launches a web browser and performs some basic functionality. This must be the future of testing and the vendors know just how to present it this way, appealing to your need to save money and time while fulfilling the testing that needs to get done.

Death of the Automation Miracle: When a testing organization gets a test automation tool for the first time, the sequence of events that follow is very common and unfortunate. Typically a QA engineer is handed a box of automation software or told about an open source tool to install and told to play around with it a bit. "This software is going to save the day" they're told "and you're the person who's going to make that happen." After an hour or two the software has been installed and a sample application has been experimented with. Sure seems at this point to live up to the promise, if only the application to automate was as simple to automate as the simple examples provided in the tutorial. Unfortunately nothing could be further from the truth, and soon most start to see just how difficult it can be to reliably interact with a real world application requiring automated testing. Countless QA organizations have test automation software installed on a computer somewhere that never saw the light of day after the initial evaluation and first attempt to use it on a real-world project. The prospect of test automation soon seems dead, expectations dashed, as the idea of the test automation magically finding all sorts of defects is lost.

What Went Wrong: I often tell those considering purchasing an automation tool to ignore nearly everything they see during the vendor demo. The reason's simple: the vendor knows the challenges involved in automating a real-world application so they demo the automation with a perfect-world application specifically built for demonstration purposes. It's been designed to enable the automation tool to easily interact with it. Additionally, most demos and automation tutorials are ridiculously simple such as opening a web browser and logging into a website. While this might mirror the most basic of test cases, it rarely comes anywhere close to the types of test that need to be automated for a real-world application. It's critical to understand this point; real-world automation is not created using a "Click-and-Record" approach no matter how much it sounds good in a sales pitch or online tutorial. Real sustainable test automation is created using sound principles of software development along with best practices in test object identification and expected results validation. Test automation has its own set of best practices including strategies for maintainability and sustainability. Ignoring these points will ensure a significant amount of effort invested with little to show for it in the long run.

Turning the Corner: Let's now consider what's necessary to turn the corner from an unrealistic approach to one that will lead to success. First is to realize that test automation is not a magic bullet, secret sauce or other miracle that simply happens because you use a great automation tool. There are test opportunities that are excellent to automate and those that are not. Foundational factors like selecting the right tool will be important. Having hired the right talent with the sufficient skill set to develop sustainable test automation will be important? Implementing an Automation Evaluation early in the process helps you to set realistic expectation as to how well your now selected tool and hired talent can reliably interact with the application under test (AUT). You will also be considering who on the team will continue to support the test automation so it stays current with application changes. Once you have successful automation in house, you might be surprised just how quickly these resources grow and how critical it is to have people in place to ensure things are backed up, updated and well managed.

Selecting a Tool: Choosing an automation tool is like purchasing a car; there are many to choose from, some better than others, some much more expensive than others. I would recommend reaching out to user groups in the area that specialize in a specific toolset. Ask how they have implemented automation and if they are reusing that automation on a regular basis. Re-usage is an important question, many will take the initial steps to try to implement automation only to abandon their efforts shortly after. When purchasing an automation tool, consider how you'll manage the developed automation scripts, which are essentially the software you have written to interact with your application under test. While they can be stored locally, they are typically stored on a server and accessed by the automation tool over the network. Make sure to implement a good backup methodology for your server to ensure automated test scripts are properly protected.

Finding the Right Automation Engineer: Regardless of the best tools you can buy, if you don't have the right talent using those tools, you may end up with a lot of time spent. I've dedicated an entire chapter (How to Hire an Automation Engineer) to the topic. Take time to read through that chapter to ensure you hire the best possible talent you can to fulfill your automation endeavors. It's important to find individuals that not only have a QA background but also have a development background. A lack in either of these areas can result in problematic test automation in my opinion.

Automation Evaluation: Performing an Automation Evaluation early in the process ensures some level of understanding about how the automation tool can interact with the application under test. This step should never be bypassed with the exception of follow-on projects. The approach to the automation evaluation is to break up the application into types of functionality, objects and other attributes that the automation tool will need to interact with. For example, one aspect of the Automation Evaluation might be to ensure the automation tool can reliably enter text within edit fields. Another part of the evaluation might ensure information can reliably be read from the screen. After each of these "Evaluation Tests" are completed, they should be scored individually on a scale from 0 to 5 based upon the results.

Automation Evaluation Scoring Scale

0 = Not Possible

1 = Complete Customized Strategy Required

2 = 80% or greater Customized Strategy Required

3 = 50% or less Customized Strategy Required

4 = 20% or less Customized Strategy Required

5 = Native Automation Tool Capabilities

The Evaluation Test should be concise and not overly complicated. Again, the purpose is to understand ahead of time where the challenges might be within the test automation effort and where things are likely to go smoothly.

* * *

A typical Evaluation Test might look something like this.

      TestName = "Button Interaction (Score = TBD)"

      '++

      'Result: Should click a button.

      '

      'Click Login button

      Result=Browser("IE").Page("Main").Button("Login").Click

      'Log Results

      Log "Pass",TestName,"Done"

* * *

Common benefits of performing an Automation Evaluation are the initial building of the Object Repository or Descriptive Programming approach. It also possible that some initial project level functions may be developed.

As a rule of thumb it's recommended to allocate two weeks for a typical Automation Evaluation. Adjust this time according to the size and complexity of the application to test. It's critical to set the expectation before the Automation Evaluation has begun, that its purpose is to determine the following:

- First, should the application be automated at all, i.e. is it a good automation candidate.
- Second, what obstacles might be encountered with the automation development?
- Third, are there areas of the application that should not be automated because they are too difficult to make reliable or the return on investment would not be met?

Set up time at the end of the Automation Evaluation to go over the individual scores and discuss the next steps. It may be that the application is an exceptional candidate for test automation with minimal areas identified as problematic. You may have the other extreme of an application that has little prospect of reliably being automated. It's a critical step to really consider is it worth the effort to automate the application at all and if so, what should be automated. The answer should never be "Everything" but instead "The Right Things".

Developing a Plan of Attack: Once an Automation Evaluation has been completed and good automation candidates have been identified, it's important to develop a plan as to what and how the automation should be developed. Consider logical breaks in the application, where automated test cases can be developed to support sub-sections of the application. Consider how automation assets (scripts, functions, objects) will be named and organized. Consider documentation and training that needs to be done to ensure the automation effort can be used going forward. The plan of attack should be incremental in its approach, where additional functionality is built out and added to over time allowing it to become more robust as time goes on.

> **Caution**: I have seen a technique used in developing automation that nearly always leads to organizational problems down the road. I do not recommend numbering automation assets as they are being developed. This method becomes problematic when additional assets need to be added at a later date. When you're deciding on an approach for organizing automated test assets, ensure its flexible enough to accommodate future growth.

Automation Development: At some point development must begin of the test automation code and following a sound methodology can really make the difference in outcome. Each automation project should be considered for the best approach. My preference is to get a very basic test case automated end-to-end so I can evaluate if the approach I have decided upon is effective. If you need to do some tweaking to your automation approach, better sooner than later. Regardless it's important to set a realistic expectation about just how long the initial test case might take to get working. Because the initial effort is being built from scratch, a significant effort is going to happen to get this first automated test case working.

The N-Curve Effect: There is a term called the "N-Curve Effect" that becomes a reality of all automation development efforts. Its basic premise is that early in a project, it will take significantly more effort to get even the most basic test cases automated but as time goes on, follow on test cases can take advantage of previous effort and test assets already developed. At some point in the project, you get to reuse more than is being built from scratch and the effort starts to not be as intense. Continuing with more and more development, you will eventually get to the peak of the N-Curve and start to come down the other side where eventually nearly all the automated test cases are built based upon existing code and little to nothing or very little new needs to be developed.

Scripted Components and Page Objects: As a rule of thumb, no single automated script should exceed a single screen or a small subset of a very complex screen. Be wary of developing a single automated script that fulfills an entire test case, this will reduce opportunities for reusability. Keep scripts to a manageable size and allocated to logical application break points. I find the best breakpoints are individual screens verse application functionality. Consider this, even the most inexperienced user can tell when they have transitioned from one screen to another but it takes someone with application experience to understand transitioning from one functional area to another.

Function Libraries: Separate function libraries into at least these two groupings, a function library specifically dedicated to the application's unique functions and a function library that is application agnostic. These are functions that are more general in purpose and can be used across multiple projects. A common mistake I see made in automation development is to locate the entire automated test case code into function libraries. Be certain you are following the prescribed approach of your automation tool when it comes to separating what should be written and stored as a function library and what should be developed as a primary scripted component. Some will opt to deviate and develop a custom approach outside how the tool was intended to be used. In most cases, I find this results in a more difficult, long term outcome when it comes to hiring and training others to support the tool. My personal rule of thumb is to use a tool as it was designed to be used and not reinvent the wheel. This approach as always yielded the best results from my experience.

Object Repository: I prefer to utilize an automation tools Object Repository (object management) functionality when at all possible. This allows a centralized method to organize and store how you will interact with the objects (Buttons, Edit Fields, etc.) of the application under test. It's important to go through a process I call "Tuning the Object Repository" where you select properties that allow reliable identification of objects and weed out the properties that provide no additional benefit. Most automation tools provide some method of identifying and building out an object management strategy. Typically more properties are included than are necessary and if not "Tuned" will lead to less reliable test automation in the long run. Utilize a consistent naming convention for types of objects such as Edit Fields, Buttons, Windows, etc. This will greatly help in code readability going forward. Adjust object nesting of sub-objects to keep the object repository organized and the object recognition responsive. Keep the object management strategy organized by screen and the objects contained on that screen. If you follow this process, you'll find it will make maintenance much easier going forward. It's also worth noting here that some automation tools do not lend themselves to a centralized object repository. Align your approach to the way the tool is designed to be used. Also consider the maintainability of the test automation you are developing. At some point, someone will need to maintain the code, so keep it as logical and consistent as possible.

Other Test Assets: Organize other test assets such as Data Sheets, Application Areas, etc. in a manner that will be easy for others to understand and follow. Make sure to remove any test assets that are no longer needed to keep the project well organized and manageable.

Internal Documentation: Ensure that code is documented as the development is happening. Identify sections of code with Begin and End notations to enable others to understand exactly what each block of code does, where it begins and ends.

Exception Handling: Building some level of exception handling into the automation code has its advantages and disadvantages. It's important to keep the perspective to bring awareness to issues encountered during the test execution. It's important to not overdo exception handling within the automation development. It's better to err on the side of the automation stalling and the execution halting then to work around an error to keep the test automation running.

> **Caution**: I have encountered test automation efforts where a good majority of the code was dedicated to exception handling. This was likely done to ensure the automation ran under any circumstance but resulted in unnecessary code and maintenance. Take time to really consider what level of exception handling is necessary.

Automation Execution: Test execution should typically be done through a test management tool (such as Quality Center). The exception to this would be during development and troubleshooting. Make sure to have your resources well organized to make it easy for others to understand and take advantage of the automation built. Put sufficient logging into your test automation to make it easier to decipher results and problems encountered during automated test execution.

Automation Maintenance: It's a good idea to "Exercise" the automation scripts on a regular basis. Even though the testing effort is completed, run automated maintenance runs on a regular basis to ensure the automation is in good working order and ready for the next project down the road. This is a great time to refine areas that need improving, add internal documentation and any other work that might have not been possible during busy development cycles.

First Steps into Test Automation

Like many QA engineers, my first introduction to test automation was based upon a tool purchased by my employer before I was hired. This tool had been sitting on the shelf, waiting for the day an unassuming QA engineer could figure out how to get some use out of it.

Soon I was facing my first project to leverage this tool and honestly, I had no idea where to begin. I clicked and recorded my way through a test case or two and tweaked the auto-generated code, resulting in my first, pieced together automation framework. Like a Rube Goldberg contraption, my automation trudged its way through test after test, helping with the need at hand but never resulting in a long term solution for our team.

Years later, with a new company, I was given that rare opportunity for a "Do-Over" and the revelation of how important it was to learn how something was intended to be used.

My employer had arranged for me to have training from the automation tool vendor. Over a week long course, we created automation to test a sample application. We drove tests with data from a spreadsheet and interacted with application objects in a variety of ways. When I completed the course, I realized the chasm of difference in how I had first used this tool in comparison to how the tool was intended to be used.

The following are tips I've learned to help make smarter steps into the world of automation. Following these will help you avoid some common pitfalls and help you get greater return on investment from your efforts.

* * *

Selecting a Tool - Choose a tool that's adaptable to a variety of environments. It should be web friendly as well as capable of interacting with typical windows objects such as buttons, form fields and gathering text. It should be capable of working with technologies such as Mobile and Service Oriented Architecture. It's reasonable to expect that you'll find a need for other tools to bridge gaps a single tool might not be able to meet. Try to keep these to what is absolutely necessary with minimal overlap if possible.

Use as Intended - Ensure you get the proper training, preferably from a credible source such as the vendor or recognized expert. You'll want to leverage the tool as it was intended to be used and not in an ad-hoc, discovered approach. This will lead you to get the most out of the tool and allow you to hire future talent that have also gone through the appropriate training, something you can look for during the hiring process. It's an unfortunate reality that much of the automation being developed these days is being done with little to no consideration for how the tool was intended to be used. This often leads to automation efforts that are not maintainable and sustainable in the long run.

Beware of the Sales Pitch - With over a decade of experience behind me, I have yet to see a "Click and Record" approach to automation that was usable for any length of time. My point, if the tool demo seems too good to be true, it probably is. Developing automation that stands the test of time requires planning and effort like any software development endeavor.

Identify Good Automation Opportunities - Contrary to popular belief, regression test cases do not always make the best automation candidates, especially for your first efforts. Consider a task your manual testers repeat over and over, processes that cover three or four steps but need to be repeated hundreds of times. These are great opportunities and help the manual test team start to identify other repetitive tasks such as environment configuration or setup that could be automated. Start simple and progress to more complex automation development.

Build a Toolbox - Develop a core library of functions that are application agnostic. I include functions that convert data, compare values, help with logging, etc. Spend time to develop these functions well as they can be utilized across numerous projects in the future. Build a separate library of functions that are application specific. Always include versioning information along with a list of included functions within each of these libraries.

Object Recognition Expertise - Become familiar with the various ways your tool interacts with application objects. All objects (Windows, Buttons, Fields, etc.) have properties that distinguish them from other similar objects. Much of the "Art" of being an automation engineer is the ability to reliably interact with various types of objects in a sea of similar objects. Avoid using methods where control keys, tabs and arrows keys are used to navigate to objects, these will prove to be unreliable in the long run.

Adoption is Important - No matter how brilliant the automation effort, if no one uses it, precious time and effort have been wasted. Build automation that serves the testing team. Start with efforts that can be completed within a week or two and monitor if this automation is getting used. Avoid extensive efforts spanning months that may lead to no adoption at all, a common reality of many ambitious automation efforts. Start small and move into more complex efforts, paying attention to adoption along the way.

The N-Curve Effect - The principal of the "N-Curve Effect" is that all automation requires some level of ramp up effort, where foundational components are put into place before the first test case can execute end to end. It can be hard to see the value of automation during the initial, steepest part of this curve much like it can be to envision the house while the foundation is being put into place. Be realistic as to how long it'll take to lay the automation foundation. Once this foundation is in place, build additional automation that leverages this foundation to get the most out of the initial efforts.

A smart plan for your automation endeavors will make a significant difference in its usefulness, adoption, and maintainability over the long haul.

Removing The Word Test From Test Automation

You initially purchased test automation tools with the idea you would automate as many test cases as possible, freeing up your manual testers for more important work. Likely that scenario panned out differently than expected but you still wound up with some test automation and a hefty price tag for the tools to develop it.

Like many technologies, test automation comes with a lot of promise of what can "easily" be done with "little to no effort". In reality, these tools take considerably more effort than promised during the sales presentation and typically yield less bang-for-the-buck at the end of the day. One reason for this ties into the perception of what test automation tools are supposed to be used for, automating tests and this is a perception I'd like to change. I've been called many things over the course of thirty years as a technologist but one reoccurring label is "Out Of the Box Thinker". Maybe it first happened the time I built a snowboard contraption and bolted it to a bicycle frame but since then, people have told me I have a way of seeing new possibilities in everyday things.

A number of years ago I was working for a large retail company in Plano,

Texas. We developed a Testing Center of Excellence (TCoE) and I was part of their test automation team. While we had developed dozens of automated testing solutions, it seemed our tool-set was capable of so much more. Then an opportunity presented itself, an in-house project needed a number of transactions put through it on a regular basis. It dawned on me that we could use our test automation tool to perform the mindless task of entering dozens of transactions as needed for our development team. Because no validation was necessary, the automation was fairly quick to build and turned out to be extremely helpful. Additionally, it gave me a glimpse of what was possible if we simply removed the word Test from Test Automation.

Now years later, I've come to realize, removing the word Test from Test Automation gives me huge advantages over many test automation engineers. I have the same tools they do but a much more open mindset to what I can do with those tools. This changed mindset allows me to bring great advantages to my company and customers and squeeze significantly more capability out of my tool-set. With this in mind, I would like to challenge you to adopt a similar way of thinking and begin referring to your Test Automation tools and Test Automation Team as simply your Automation Tools and Team. Consider you've now officially taken this first step and read on to learn some amazing opportunities right around the corner, utilizing your tools and resources in ways you've never considered before.

***

Automated Transaction Entry - Identify repetitive tasks happening within your organization that could be automated. Remove the idea that you have to test something along the way, just consider repetitive things that happen on a regular basis and determine if you can automate them. Ensure you pick opportunities that build upon themselves and are not significantly different from one another. Target automation opportunities that can be completed within a few weeks and that will be used every month, weekly or even daily if possible. Finding good wins in areas like these can free up talented people for greater creative opportunities.

Automated Data Validation - I came across a project like this a number of years ago, a single website containing over 10,000 values to validate. Even the most determined test engineer would be fatigued when trying to validate a volume of data like this. Instead, we leveraged our automation tool to complete this task in less than an hour, freeing our testers to focus on more complex tasks. Identify opportunities within your organization that have very repetitive tasks, where manual testers only validate a small portion due to the scope and size of what ultimately needs to be validated. Consider areas where no user interface exists yet where your automation tool can make countless SQL calls to validate actual results against expected results. See my White Paper on the SQE website regarding working with Complex Data for some tools and ideas in moving forward with these types of opportunities.
http://www.stickyminds.com/presentation/automation-strategies-testing-complex-data-and-dashboards

Automated Environment Validation/Configuration The capabilities of even the most basic automation tools will allow you to check for directories and files that exist on a local file system. With minimal additional effort, registry entries can be validated and even set. Explore within your organization the need to ensure environments are set up in specific ways. See if you can identify the parameters one would want to verify to make sure a testing or development environment are set up in a specific way. Since most automation tools can launch applications, it's possible to have the automation tool open up multiple applications and ensure they are properly configured.

Automated System Monitoring - Have you ever considered that an extra PC laying around the office could be re-purposed to monitor whether or not a variety of systems are online and working as expected? In addition to monitoring, the automation could email, text or open a ticket with support services if something was determined to be down. Sure there are other types of technologies that can do this but if you're on a tight budget, already own automation software, and simply want an easy way to monitor things, an inexpensive PC doing this type of work could be a real lifesaver.

Automated Data Preparation/Setup - How often do you need unique test data? Consider the capabilities of your automation tool to generate test data for your organization as needed and in specific formats and quantities. Seeding programmatic arrays with data using a random number generator could lead to some very creative data generation capabilities.

Combine the mathematical and string capabilities of your automation tools and you could generate addresses, zip codes, pricing and tax data for all sorts of applications. Whether it's random data or data that follows a prescribed methodology, allowing your automation to be an effective tool for generating test data makes good sense.

> **Tip**: A new technique I've started to use to identify automation opportunities (AutoOpps as I call them) is to schedule regular desk visits with my Test Engineers to learn what's eating their lunch. This has resulted in countless AutoOpps identified in just a few short months. Make sure to come up with a method to document the AutoOpps you identify so they can be evaluated regularly and developed as time allows. Regularly evaluate theses AutoOpps for applicability to current challenges and leverage capabilities learned and developed in earlier AutoOpp development projects. Keep AutoOpp development to no more than two weeks of time per opportunity if possible.

Like Albert Einstein who stepped back from things to ask "What would it be like to travel a beam of light" which yielded his remarkable Theory of Relativity, take time to step back and think outside the box of classic Test Automation. If you do, I'm certain you'll uncover great opportunities right under the surface of everyday life in the day of a typical Quality Assurance engineer.

As Designed vs. As Discovered

I decided to include this chapter to provide some food for thought on an important topic. Are you one of those people who strive to do things in excellence? Do you take your time calculating your next move before actually taking it? If so then read on...

I want to share with you a thinking exercise I went through when considering why we use tools the way we do. If you're reading this book, then it stands to reason you either already have some automation tool(s) or are considering implementing some in the future.

After many years of interacting with individuals developing test automation, I started to notice something that's caught my attention. I discovered major automation efforts, many coming close to a year's worth of development, yielding ineffective, unreliable results. On reflecting why these individuals were having such trouble creating effective, reliable test automation, I identified one outstanding characteristic: they had learned to use the toolset through a discovery process or were taught by someone who had simply figured a way to use it by trial and error. This approach seemed to consistently yield less than favorable results and often yielded abandoned automation efforts altogether.

What I came to learn is a phrase I share with new automation engineers when I mentor them, "Use a tool as Designed not as Discovered". The heart of this statement is that most things have been created with an intent and purpose in mind. Attributes, features and capabilities have been added in the creation process to take a good idea and make it better. Make sure you take time to learn how your automation tool is intended to be used. This will lead to getting the most out of the tool. Be wary of hiring automation engineers that have simply pieced their knowledge together through trial and error. Be sure to allocate training into the budget so you can be certain you're getting the most from your tools you purchase and adopt.

Below is a thinking exercise I went through to help consider this point further and to understand the repercussions of ignoring this idea of using a tool as designed.

* * *

When writing this book, I pulled many resources from writings I have done over the years. These included lessons learned and in this case, an analysis I went through to better understand the realities of using a tool based upon the way it was designed to be used vs. figuring it out through a process of discovery. I decided to include that analysis here for your interest. Enjoy!

An analysis in considering **As Designed** vs. **As Discovered**

A tool should be used **As Designed**.

When a tool is not used as designed, it is used **As Discovered**.

Using a tool **As Discovered** may lead to some new opportunities such as innovation, extended capability, or a broader range of usage.

Using a tool **As Discovered** has a greater opportunity to lead to not using that tool **As Designed**.

The more complex a tool is, the more likely a tool being used **As Discovered** will lead further away from the way to tool was intended to be used **As Designed**.

Using a tool **As Designed** is more likely to yield efficient results because the intent for how the tool was to be used was factored into its design.

Using a tool **As Discovered** has greater potential to introduce risk because the tool may not have the proper attributes, capabilities to scale, work long term, operate safely or economically in the **As Discovered** direction.

Traceability back to a credible source, instructing in the use of a tool **As Designed** is critical when teaching and mentoring others in the usage of a that tool **As Designed**.

Teaching and Mentoring others in the usage of a tool without traceability to a credible source can lead to greater misuse, risk and waste in the usage of that tool and perpetuates the problem each successive cycle.

* * *

Some parting thoughts on this topic: Of course there is a time for discovery of most tools once a foundation has been put into place and you begin to use a tool as it was designed. Then things get interesting as you now consider new ways to get even greater usage out of your tools.

The Automation Evaluation

"Well can't we just automate everything?" These were the words from our internal customer! Fortunately my manager had enough experience with test automation to know how unassuming those words were and how easily they could get us into big trouble.

If you're a Test Automation Engineer or Quality Assurance Engineer, you're bound to hear these words eventually, "We'll just automate the entire regression suite". For some of us, that's what led us to our first test automation job and for others it was the beginning of trying to fulfill "The Automation Miracle". Once you start walking down this road, trying to automate everything thrown at you, the reality starts to set in that this is anything but smart. It will put food on the table, for a while at least but in the end, it's an unrealistic approach to building successful test automation. For this very reason, I started to add an "Automation Evaluation" into the beginning of every potential automation project proposed.

In a nutshell, an Automation Evaluation is simply a way to determine what should be automated and how that automation should be built. It's a critical step in setting realistic expectations with your customer instead of trying to automate everything, regardless of it being a good automation candidate or not. If you're a QA Manager or IT Manager is looking to hire someone to build your test automation, you should request an Automation Evaluation to be done before every major effort is started. Analyze the results and be wary of anyone who tells you they will automate everything, you are positively going to throw good money down the drain.

So what goes into a good Automation Evaluation?

How long should it take to complete one?

What should you expect from the results of an Automation Evaluation?

* * *

Smart steps to an effective Automation Evaluation:

Select a Basic Test Case: In order to perform an Automation Evaluation, start by selecting a simple test case. This test case should traverse through a typical "Happy Path" of your application. It should bring the Automation Engineer in contact with typical application objects such as Windows, Dialogs, Edit Fields, Drop Down Menus, Buttons, etc. It's important that the most common types of objects found within the application will be encountered through this basic test case.

> **Note**: I commonly ask a manual tester to perform the basic test case while using a screen capture tool to record a movie of the

manual steps being performed. Later I'll take that movie and save individual screen shots, which I assemble into a basic flowchart.

These initial steps allow you to consider how the application will be broken up into automated components (such as reusable actions); one screen per component is the method I recommend. This is also a great time to consider the naming convention you'll use for components, object, variables, etc. Putting this groundwork in now is a great first step to an Automation Evaluation.

Build a Data Strategy: Step through the movie recorded in the earlier step and document all the data needed to fulfill the entire test case. I suggest using a spreadsheet for this process. Organize the spreadsheet screen-by-screen, placing "|" pipe characters in their own, individual columns to designate when you've transitioned from one screen to the next. By using this screen-by-screen organization method, you make it very easy to understand what data goes with each screen and it'll make it much easier to maintain your automation data in the long run. Consider the naming you're using to identify and describe this data. This naming is typically entered in the first row of a spreadsheet and is what most automation tools will use to reference specific test data. These data value references should have some preceding identifier, indicating the screen they are related to. This is one area I will use some abbreviation such as "LIUsername" referencing the Login Page and Username Field and "LIPassword" for the Password Field. Go through each screen and document all the data value references and actual data, going back through the data strategy to adjust it for intuitiveness and readability.

> **Note**: Although it may seem like a good idea to shorten or abbreviate the user interface names in the data strategy, in the long run this typically adds more work for the person who has to maintain it down the road.

Plugin and Configuration Optimizing: The next step is to ensure that the optimum configuration of Test Automation is in place. Verify that plugins and configuration settings are accurate for the technology of the application you're testing. Never assume the configuration you've used before is the same for the next application you're automating. Developers can replicate a look and feel from one technology while leveraging a completely different technology. Meet with your developers and ask about any specialized dependencies such as browser plugins, java dependencies, etc. These will each have their optimum configuration, which ensures your test automation can clearly and effectively control the application being tested. This part of the Automation Evaluation will give you insight as to what your automation tool is capable of manipulating and where it might have challenges.

> **Note**: I've encountered objects that resembled ones I had interacted with countless times before. Then in a future automation effort I came across objects that visually looked identical yet my automation tool was nearly blind to them.

As you encounter difficult to interact with objects, be certain to document them in the Automation Evaluation. Be certain to document if they are in the critical path of future test automation efforts and if there are any reasonable alternatives.

> **Note**: I find some of the more difficult objects to work with will require developing custom functions to interact with them. Try to identify these early on, before committing to build a bunch of test automation that might end up brittle in the end.

Object Identification: Now build your object identification strategy. I prefer to use a centralized object repository where I can manage my entire object library from one common source.

> **Note**: Many test automation tools require instantiating (launching) the application to be automated from within the test automation tool. This allows the automation tool to put a type of "wrapper" around the application, a way for it to see the application well. Make sure you are using the approach that gives to the greatest visibility to the objects you will be examining for your object strategy.

Begin to manually navigate to the very first screen identified in your flowchart. Analyze every object and its unique properties that are included in the test case. Think about your naming convention; plan for growth and scaling, organizing objects based upon a screen-by-screen approach. What you're trying to determine is how easy or difficult it is for your automation tool to successfully interact with the application.

Now that you've completed one screen, move on to the next. Don't worry about the automation code at this time, just the objects required to fulfill the basic test case. You should be noticing a pattern to the types of object properties that are necessary to reliably interact with each object. A good rule of thumb in object identification is to find one to two unique properties for each object. In a rare case, utilizing regular expressions is necessary but should be avoided unless there is no other option. Also be aware of using any type of "Smart Identification" with object recognition. "Smart Identification" allows the automation tool to try to determine how to identify the object and typically is not reliable over the long haul. Try to avoid using any sort of "Index" numbering unless there is no other alternative to identifying an object. This approach will be problematic in any future updates where additional similar objects are added to the user interface.

Go screen-by-screen, following your flowchart through the entire test case. Organize and group your objects based upon an individual screen. Don't worry about redundancy of common objects such as "OK" buttons, etc. In the end you want each group of objects to support all the objects for a single screen.

Automation Code: By now, you're probably chomping at the bit to build some test automation code. Start back at the first steps of the test case. Build the basic functionality, reading values from the data strategy (spreadsheet) as you need them. Include any indexing and looping mechanisms that allow you to increment one row at a time, one row, one test case. The main script I tend to start off with is one I commonly refer to as the "Stub" script. It drives all the automation going forward. It has the ability to read data from the data strategy and send the automation off into any direction necessary to fulfill any test case.

> **Note**: Later on, you can add code to the Stub script to validate the environment is in proper working order such as servers available, databases online, etc. The Stub script concept has many useful capabilities.

Work your way screen-by-screen, component (reusable action) by component until the test case automation is built. As you're debugging the test execution, you'll likely encounter challenges that are common to most automation efforts. The most common of these will likely be synchronization issues. Take time to develop a strong synchronization strategy during your Automation Evaluation. Identify reliable ways to know a page is fully loaded, that objects are enabled or disabled, that objects exist or are non-existent. These are worth the effort now to understand how they will be handled.

Note: Be cautious of using any type of "Wait()" statement to add delays into your test automation for synchronization purposes. If you're unaware of using Exist() or other types of synchronization strategies, now is the time to learn them. This will make the difference in long-term results of your test automation efforts.

Test and Tune: Now that you have one test case automated, run and run again this single automated test. Run it remotely from your test management tool if you have one. Run it against different browsers and environments. Use this time to identify any trouble areas that need to be understood and reworked. By now you should have a really good feel for how reliable the test automation will be and what level of effort is required to complete automating a single test case.

Report Findings: You should now be ready to report your findings to those requesting the automation to be built. Include what worked and more importantly, where you encountered problems. This is the time you want to set the expectation, if you should continue the automation effort and with what specific strategy. This information should provide a better idea of the cost in time and money for you to move forward with the project. They should know what they're getting into and if any risk to reliability exists. Remember to set the expectation of what it will take to maintain the automation going forward. This is a great time to share the data strategy you've developed and present the flowchart showing the basic framework that you propose to build.

Some final thoughts on Automation Evaluations: In most cases, a typical Automation Evaluation can be completed in a few weeks. This will need to be adjusted if the application is overly complex but is reasonable for most. If you're a Test Automation Engineer looking to start a new job, ask the QA/Automation manager their thoughts on performing an Automation Evaluation.

Art and Soul of a Function Library

I remember the first automation script I wrote many years ago. I was amazed that it was possible to write software to interact with software. With that knowledge, I wrote hundreds of lines of code that could navigate and interact with a basic application. Eventually I realized, test automation development was actually software development and that meant there was an art to doing it well.

Most automation engineers start the same way I did; they develop some code that traverses its way through an application, fulfilling some or all of the parts of a manual test case. Eventually the realization sets in that writing the same code over and over again would be better accomplished by building a single function.

So what's a function you might be asking? A function is a software code snippet that fulfills a specific purpose. It might perform a complex calculation or compare two values but functions in general fulfill some task that needs to be performed over and over again.

With years of experience behind me, I have come to realize a well thought out function can be the difference in writing a great, automated solution or ending up with a maintenance nightmare. Combining a group of well-designed functions into a function library gives the automation engineer an arsenal of capability. It's easy to get fixated on the task of building test automation and never consider future projects. It's important for a QA Manager to encourage their Automation Engineers to step back from the project and ask the question "Will I have need to perform similar functionality like this in the future?" This type of thinking will lead to seeing the value of building a great function library.

I like to view the world of function libraries in two categories. The first are functions specific to an application being tested. This type of library will have very specialized functions that would do little good if they were used in a different application. The second type of function library is application agnostic. Functions in this library can be used across most automation endeavors and have nothing specific to an application within their libraries. That's it, two categories of function libraries, **Application Specific** and **Application Agnostic**.

Before we go much further, let me share with you a naming convention I use for all my function libraries. This naming convention has stood the test of time and I use it consistently across all my automation efforts.

Let's assume I have an application named Bill Organizer and am setting up the function libraries that will house the reusable code to be used across this automation project. Every project will have access to at least two function libraries; this is how they would be named.

> FL_BillOrganizer (Application Specific)
> FL_Core (Application Agnostic)

I now have all the necessary function libraries in place to begin the project. As I go through the development process and come across opportunities to develop functions, I ask this important question, does this function only support this one application (Application Specific) or can it be used in future projects (Application Agnostic).

Each function library has the same internal format allowing the capturing of overall versioning of the function library and cataloging the content of the library. This really comes in handy, especially with the FL_Core (Application Agnostic) library, which can grow to many thousands of lines of code.

This example shows the typical header of a function library.

```
'================================================================
'Function Library FL_Core
'
'Version 1.04
'
'Description:
'Core functions commonly needed for automation.
'Additional functions added here if Application Agnostic.
'
'Functions Included:
'   StringCounter(SearchString, SearchChars)
'   PercentCalc(CurrentVal, MaxVal)
'   FileExist(Filename, Filepath)
'
'Revision History
'   v1.00 - Initial version (04/16/2014) GP
'   v1.01 - Added StringCounter function (05/15/2014) GP
'   v1.02 - Updated StringCounter function (05/20/2014) GP
'   v1.03 - Added PercentCalc function (06/12/2014) GP
'   v1.04 - Added FileExist function (07/09/2014) GP
'================================================================
```

Now that we have a place and process to determine what functions will go in which library, let's talk about the specific anatomy of a function within the function library. The example I provide here is one I have used for years and find very effective.

```
'****************************************************
'Function Name StringCounter
'Description This function counts string occurrences
'Parameters SearchString - String with characters to count
'            SearchChars - Character to search for
'Return Value Number of characters counted
'****************************************************
Function StringCounter(SearchString, SearchChars)
   '+++ Declarations Begin +++
   'Variables
    Dim Result
   '++++++++++++++++++++

   'Prepare the Strings
   StringCount = 0

Result=Len(SearchString)-Len(Replace(SearchString,SearchChars,""))

   'Set Return Value
   StringCounter = Result

   '- - - Disassociation Begins - - -
   'Variables
    Set Result = Nothing
   'Objects
    'N/A
   '- - - - - - - - - - - - - - - -
End Function
```

This function provides very clear identifiers as to where it begins and ends. I like to think of it as a block and have found this approach makes for easy maintenance in the long run.

Within the function block is a header area containing important details such as the Description, Parameters and details on how to utilize the function. In the body of the function you'll find adequate details as to what is happening within the function. At the beginning and end of the function there should be code declaring and releasing variables and objects. I often use (Begin) and (End) remarks to identify sections of the code, again to aid in easier maintenance. There are certain variables I reuse commonly across most functions such as the variable "Result". The trick in all this is to be as consistent as possible in designing your functions. You need to assume that someone other than yourself will have to maintain this code somewhere down the road. Even if it's you maintaining the code, 6 or 12 months from now, it will probably not look familiar to you.

Now that you know about two function libraries you should include in every automation effort, let's talk about additional libraries that might have a place in your project. There will be a point in your automation career where you realize you are working with a certain type of technology or solving a specific type of problem that likely will reoccur somewhere down the road. I call these specialized libraries and they are still Application Agnostic but not necessary a good fit for the FL_Core library. I have a handful of libraries like this such as FL_Datasheet, FL_Validation, FL_ComplexData, etc. These libraries typically come out of very specialized projects where you need to work within a specific type of technology. It's not uncommon to build these specialized libraries and then utilize them a few projects down the road and enhance them with additional functions.

So what goes into creating a great function? Let's talk specifically building your FL_Core library. Remember, these are functions that you plan on using over and over again. They are not tied to any specific technology (Web, Client, etc.) but meant to be very generic in nature. Take time to build really solid functions. Consider the parameters you include as inputs and consider if there are other, obvious additional parameters that will be needed in future projects. Add them now instead of waiting later is my advice. I personally find my FL_Core library to be solid, and it rarely needs additional parameters added to existing functions. I do find opportunities to refine the internal workings of a function but do my best to not add parameters or change their order once it's committed to the FL_Core library. One approach I take, when a function will likely end up in the FL_Core library but is not yet mature is to include it in my FL_Application (e.g. FL_BillOrganizer) library. Once it's matured, then it gets migrated to the FL_Core library. Just keep in mind that once it's committed to the FL_Core library, it should be thoroughly debugged and ready to stand the test of time. Take time to make these functions, masterpieces.

* * *

Now I want to turn to some of the common mistakes I see made in function libraries and why you should avoid these.

Beware of making a bunch of function libraries. Seriously, I have seen this many times, an automation project with twenty function libraries. This approach almost always comes from trying to add some level of organization to the function libraries that is unnecessary. It's an ineffective approach and one that will come at a high cost during maintenance.

Imagine you've just been hired into a company to help work on their test automation. You adopt a project that was automated years ago. The code needs updating and it's obvious something is broken in a function. If you have twenty function libraries to search through and you are unfamiliar with the application, it would be a lesson in frustration. The automation engineer that set this up probably had the best of intentions, but this approach never results in an easy to maintain automation endeavor. It's likely all the Application Specific functions could have been located into the FL_Application library and been much easier to maintain in the future.

There is a myth that having a large function library can slow your test execution down; this is simply not true. Keep your function library inventory to two if possible and unless you have a FL_Specilized (e.g. FL_Datasheet) library, you should not have any need to add others.

Be careful of forgetting to document your functions at the time of development. Most well-meaning automation engineers have done this when it to comes crunch time to get the project wrapped up. Most swear they will add the documentation later, but that rarely turns out to be the case. This will become a pain when it's time to maintain the automation down the road, especially if the project is handed over to someone less familiar with the initial effort.

* * *

Writing great functions is so much more than clever code development. Building in the ability for it to be easy to understand and maintain are the marks of a great function library. Start by investing in an FL_Core library, it will become one of your most valuable assets as an automation engineer.

How to Hire an Automation Engineer

So you've decided to go ahead and jump into the deep end and hire a test automation engineer. In this chapter I want to share some critical steps in finding and hiring a great test automation engineer. Let me start off by saying that not all automation engineers are created equal. The field of Test Automation is full of "Automation Experts" that have years of automation development in their hip pocket but may not be the right candidate you are looking for. The honest truth is most automation engineers you'll interview will be self-taught or possibly taught by another automation engineer who was self-taught. Unfortunately, very few automation engineers have formal training and that presents a number of challenges.

> **Reality Check:** Should you hire someone with years of experience, because they have built some form of automation in their past? Would it make better sense to hire an individual with the right, fundamental skill set and then arrange for them to take training from a reputable source on the specific tools you own? Most automation engineers (and

manual testers) you'll interview will have some previous experience of test automation in their portfolio. This is one of those professional fields that nearly anyone can claim they have experience in yet it's hard to actually know the quality of product they are capable of creating.

It's critical to have a strategy for identifying and hiring a great automation engineer. Their skills and talents must be mature enough to ensure you end up with maintainable, sustainable test automation that can be used over the long haul. Well-trained automation engineers will put into place proper software development methodology, documentation and training to ensure you'll get long term benefit from their efforts. An individual lacking training and proven, successful automation projects should not lead your automation efforts. This reality of having untrained individuals piece together test automation and worse, a framework, will result in test automation that does not scale, is hard to maintain and typically fails within the first year or two.

ROI Reality Check: Did you know it typically takes 6-12 months to develop an automation framework? Realizing **Return on Investment** (ROI) for most frameworks takes multiple reuses over a number of years to justify building it in the first place. Don't be misled by "Click and Record" marketing hype, real world test automation is a software development endeavor.

Here are some key characteristics to look for when hiring a great automation engineer for your organization.

Bring along some help: If you're the hiring manager yet don't have enough experience to understand software development terms, consider asking one of your software developers to join you during the interview process. They can be an invaluable source of insight into the candidate's technical capabilities.

* * *

Key talents and abilities to look for in finding a great Automation Engineer:

1. Development Background: Experienced in programming languages such as Visual Basic, JavaScript, C, PERL, etc. would be preferable. Many automation tools use simple scripting languages such as VBScript and fortunately, most languages follow similar syntax usage and can easily be picked up by those who have developed software before in other languages. Ask to see a code sample they've written in the past and have them explain the basics of what it does. You're looking for a candidate that understands coding principals well and can proceed with the work, self-directed.

2. Quality Assurance Background: It's useful to find a candidate who has a Quality Assurance background. Yes that's going to make it more difficult to find a candidate but you'll be hiring an individual that understands the test automation they're developing is actually testing another software product. By the way, I've seen automation engineers lose sight of this fact and focus solely on ensuring their test automation executes, at any cost. They forget the fundamental point that their automation software's purpose is to perform testing.

3. Interest in Documenting: Look for a candidate who can provide examples, showing well-organized and documented code. You want to see logical breaks and annotations that will help others that would need to update and make additions to the code. Be wary of those that don't document but promise to do so for your project. The natural inclination to document shows their capability to step back from the code now and again and review the work that's been completed. If they don't document when you first meet them, they likely won't document once they're part of your team. Find a candidate that places value in documenting their code.

4. **Simplicity over Complexity**: In the software development world, there lies a temptation to show off just how "brilliant" one is. Most often this shows up in extremely complex coding practices, where functionality is overly nested within other functionality making it hard to follow and maintain. Let's face it, there are times when this approach is appropriate but it should not be the predominate method used throughout the automation development. Identify manageable groups of functionality in code examples that perform a specific task. Look for a rhythm in the code development; my preferred method typically follows verifying the state of an application followed by the action to be performed. You should see sufficient logging happening making it easier to maintain this code in the long run. Again remember, automation development is software development. Find someone who has a mature skill set.

5. **Success Stories**: If you're interviewing a candidate who has developed automation in the past, ask them to tell you about a number of successful projects they've completed. The success should not simply be the completion of the project but should include the reuse of the test automation code over many years. You're trying to get an understanding

of their mindset when it comes to developing test automation for the long haul. No test automation is really considered successful until it has been used multiple times over a number of years. An unfortunate reality is that many times, automation is developed for a project and never used again. You'll want a candidate who understands the importance of re-usability in their automation efforts.

6. **Learns from Failure**: While no one wants to deliberately experience a failure in the work they do, the reality is that "stuff happens". There will be those projects that don't yield the results initially intended. Fortunately though, these scenarios hold a great opportunity for a wise automation engineer. It's oftentimes through failure that we learn our greatest lessons and which help to teach us to approach a problem differently the next go around. Ask the individual for an example where a project did not go as planned and what came about from the experience. A smart individual will be reflective on the results and identify lessons they learned and took away from the experience.

7. **Teachable Attitude**: Consider how teachable the individual is: would they be willing to learn from the efforts of others? Consider their attitude towards teaching others: would they willingly communicate what they're learning to others? Would they strive to make sure others understood what they were trying to communicate even if that required taking a different approach? A teachable attitude is particularly valuable for the automation lead that will be mentoring junior automation engineers. Their ability to model this characteristic to other team members

will bring exponential benefits, encouraging others to share what they're learning as well. Be cautious of ego-centered individuals who might belittle younger engineers needing guidance.

8. **Reputable Training**: Finding an automation engineer trained by a reputable source means your new team member has the skills to use the automation tool as it is intended to be used. One of the most common issues encountered with automation engineers is they have not had any training on the tools they use every day. This leaves them to either learn from someone who has had the appropriate vendor training (very rare) or (more often) figure out a methodology all on their own or by someone who also learned it on their own. In most cases, the latter is the reality, which yields to some bizarre automation methodologies, where sustainability and maintainability are rarely considered. If you're hiring an automation lead or building a new automation team, be sure to budget for a number of your team members to get reputable training, it will make a difference in the automation they will develop. If you purchase a commercial, off the shelf tool, the best solution is to purchase training directly from the tool vendor. If you have decided to utilize an Open Source tool such as Selenium, look for training from a trusted source, which could include published materials from a leader in that toolset. Either purchasing training from the tool vendor or a trusted leader in the toolset you have selected, realize, you are learning not only the tool but also the methodology for using that tool well.

* * *

Here is a list of red flags to look for, indicating the potential for problems when hiring an Automation Engineer.

1.   Click and Record: If at any time during the interview process you hear the words "Click and Record" or "Record and Playback", you would be wise to dig in further and find out more about their usage of these words. Click and Record is only really valid during the sales presentation and possibly during learning how to use test automation tools. Real World test automation is never (yes I did say never) developed using Click and Record techniques. If you have a candidate that insist this is the approach they've used in the past, then this would be a candidate you should pass on.

2.   Automation Hocus-Pocus: Are you hearing about results that seem a little too good to be true? Unfortunately, the test automation world is full of this type of promise. Chick and Record, Write Once Run Everywhere, Smart Object Recognition, and other terms are as much hocus-pocus as they sound. Most of these terms might work in a sales presentation but will not result in test automation efforts that will scale and be useful for multiple years and multiple product releases. Follow your gut during the interview process and be aware of those automation endeavors that seem too good to be true.

ROI Robbers in Test Automation

"ROI (Return on Investment) Robbers" are seen in many engineering endeavors where "Best Practices" are either unknown or ignored and result in a finished product that's less than what's possible. QA organizations see this most often in their efforts to develop test automation. Individuals are tasked with creating automated scripts that replicate manual tests. They're rarely given formal training and often lack real world experience that produces results in software testing.

As discussed in this book, the first steps to ensuring ROI Robbers don't enter your automation effort is to hire experienced, Automation Engineers to begin with. They should have a successful software development track record and preferably, a background in Quality Assurance. Two extremes can result when hiring individual lacking one of these two critical skill sets.

QA Engineer with no software development experience - Typically results in an unorthodox automation approach that may fulfill test case execution but rarely ends up as maintainable, sustainable test automation. This is typically realized within the first few years of automation development, when others are required to maintain and execute the automation on an ongoing basis.

Software Development Engineer with no QA experience - Typically results in automation development that fulfills the test case steps regardless of the quality of the application. This "come hell or high water" approach is easy to slip into when the goal no longer becomes testing software quality but instead focuses on the number of test cases automated or getting the automation to fulfill the test case by whatever means necessary.

Both scenarios can be traps for even the most veteran Automation Engineer. Do the following to help with these problems.

1. Put into place a "Reality Check" to ensure the automation being developed is maintainable and sustainable for the long haul.
2. Regularly verify that the test automation is actually validating the quality of the application under test.

The following are real world ROI Robbers that sneak their way into many test automation efforts across a variety of tool-sets and methodologies. While raising awareness of these ROI Robbers, I'll provide some resolutions to help remove these problems if they already exist in your test automation.

* * *

Common ROI Robbers:

1 - Over-Abstraction - This is a fundamental problem most automation tools seem to encourage. Over abstraction simply means to add more complexity to solving a problem than is actually necessary. Like the famous Rube Goldberg machines seen in old comic strips, over abstraction means your automation is simply more complicated than it needs to be.

Identification - Test data spread across multiple spreadsheets and tabs. Look for automation components broken down by individual objects instead of by screen or logical groupings. Find function libraries broken into countless, excessive libraries. If your gut is telling you "This seems a little more complicated than I expected" then you're likely identifying a case of over-abstraction. Many well-meaning Automation Engineers can lead you down this road without even realizing it or not identifying the problem until it's too late. This is a good one to catch earlier than later as it can really be difficult to reverse out of a fully built automation framework.

Resolution – For test data over abstractions, locate test data to fulfill a single test case onto one row of a spreadsheet. Group data by screen and use a pipe "|" character in its own cell to indicate where one screen's data ends and another begins. Resist breaking test data into multiple tabs and worse, multiple spreadsheets. Consider the long term in managing test data and easily adding to it in the future. While the single row of data per test case may be long, in the end you'll find it's easier to maintain. When it comes to components, keep the ratio of one automated component to one screen. As stated before regarding function libraries, two are typically all that are needed. One to contain all functions specific to the application, the other to contain application agnostic functions you continue to build and use in future projects.

2 - "With" Statements - Some popular test automation tools provide a programming syntax called "With". The "With" statement is a type of coding shortcut to make interacting with objects less complicated. The way "With" statements are typically implemented is to surround a block of code using the "With" statement. Anything inside this "With" statement block assumes certain objects are already being referenced. Using "With" statements makes it harder to maintain and troubleshoot code if it's not easy to identify the original objects it referenced. This is made worse if the "With" statement is defined hundreds of lines of code above from where the automation engineer is currently maintaining or adding new code. This will require them to hunt down the initial "With" statement to understand the root object path. In the end, I've rarely seen "With" statements worth implementing, so stay away from using them if possible.

Identification - "With" statements are easy to identify because you will actually see the word "With" included in the automation code. You'll also find object references that simply begin with a period (e.g. .but_OK).

Resolution - Remove all "With" statements and restore your code to the full object paths. This does result in more code but adds maintainability to thing, ensuring the code is simpler to manage in the future.

3 - Hard Coded Data - Hard coded data, file paths and other potentially static values, typically solve an immediate need but introduce problems later down the road. Consider values you are working with in your test automation. Are they environment specific? If your automation were required to run in another environment, would these values need to be updated? When you begin to lay the groundwork for a new automation framework, put into place a methodology for managing values that are needed across the automation but could change in the future. I often simply include these in my data strategy and while they rarely change, they bring great benefit when the time comes to change them. A simple tweak to the data in my datasheet and we're up and running in a completely different environment, with different users and other values. It's easy to get into the mindset of "If we ever need to run this automation on another environment, we'll simply update the code for that environment." This shortsighted thinking has plagued many an automation framework. In a recent example, I encountered a framework that could only be executed on one test environment, on a single machine by one individual.

Identification - Look for numbers, file paths, URL's and other values that tie the automation to a specific environment, machine or user. Consider where you might use the automation in the future and if these values would need to be changed.

Resolution - Move hard coded values into your data strategy. In most cases, this will be your datasheet. Be careful not to over-abstract your automation, moving data across multiple datasheets and tabs. Keep things simple while still providing flexibility to accommodate future changes.

4 - Environment Variables - An environment variable provides a way to designate a value that is accessible across the automation framework. They can be useful in very limited usage but often are misused by not understanding basic programming concepts such as function parameters and return values. Personally, I never use environment variables; I believe all data should be handled by the data strategy. Nonetheless, I do believe limited usage of environment variables is acceptable if they are limited, located and managed in a way that is easy to maintain.

Identification - Look for environment variables created within functions and subroutines implemented to pass values to other areas of the code. If you find yourself tempted in this way, consider the scope of your function. Is it too large, performing too much functionality? I think a root cause of automation engineers using environment variables to pass values around the framework is they don't understand the difference between functions and subroutines. When I interview potential automation engineers, I often ask them this question to see how well they understand the basic fundamentals of programming concepts such as functions and subroutines.

Resolution - Functions and Subroutines should have no dependencies on environment variables. Inexperienced automation engineers may utilize subroutines (which do not pass back a value to the calling code) instead of functions, which will pass back a return result. Consider simplifying the design, breaking functions into smaller segments, passing back values to the calling code. Convert subroutines to functions if you see environment variables used to pass values back to the calling code.

5 - Code Duplication - Code duplication introduces many challenges, the biggest being consistent maintainability of the automation framework. I've encountered a number of situations where you resolve a bug in the automation in one place only to see it show up later in some other place. The concept of Functions, Subroutines, Reusable Actions and Business Components was designed in part to alleviate code duplication.

Identification - These are typically easy to find, as you will see the identical code, variables and all, in multiple locations. Look for multiple function libraries or code snippets performing identical functionality.

Resolution - Consider how duplicate code can be centralized in a function library. Keep functions concise in what they do.

6 - Undocumented Code - There's no better time to document your code than when your building it. So often code documenting is an afterthought that never gets implemented or it's so vague it provides no help to those needing to maintain the code.

Identification - It's easy to spot undocumented code as you'll find none or minimal internal remarks. Additionally see if code is indented properly, this will add much readability and make it easier to maintain.

Resolution - First start by properly indenting and inserting spaces to make the code more readable. As you're going through the code line by line, include details as to what various loops, function calls and other sections of the code are doing.

7 - Unconventional Looping Practices - The ability to understand code flow including loops, conditionals, etc. is important for maintainability. Most programmers needing to maintain your code will expect you to use typical conventions in exiting loops. If you need to exit a loop, set the loop counter to the maximum value and allow the loop to end gracefully. Avoid force exiting a loop in ways that break the flow of code execution.

Identification - Look for end of function or return calls within loops, forcing them to exit before the remaining code completes. Look for exiting Do and For loops outside the met condition of the loop. Keep an eye out for Exit If and Exit Do commands.

Resolution - Exit loops gracefully. If the loop is designed to exit on certain criteria, set that criteria when the condition is met and allow the loop to complete its execution. This allows any subsequent code for cleanup to be executed properly.

8 - Unconventional Error Handling - When it comes to Error handling, I personally prefer to have the automation fail (run off the tracks) than try to anticipate all the possible scenarios it could encounter. I've seen many automation frameworks contain more error handling code than the code to fulfill the primary testing functionality. Does it really make sense to be investing so much time in code that will rarely execute? Keep your error handling to only what's absolutely necessary.

Identification - Look for On Error usage in the automation framework. Are you seeing a pattern of it being used everywhere? Some automation developers include On Error Resume Next in hopes that the automation will stumble its way through the execution of the test case. This approach makes it difficult to identify what needs refactoring for greater reliability.

Resolution - Keep error handling to an absolute minimum. There will be cases when it's necessary such as checking for the existence of a file or other checks that might deliberately produce an error. Never blanket your test automation with On Error simply to avoid the automation from stalling. Better to have it "Run Off the Tracks" and fix the problem than to pretend it never happened.

9 - Unconventional Object Recognition - Most automation tools have a methodology for managing and identifying objects that will be interacted with. In the tool-set I use, this is known as the Object Repository. A secondary approach is to use a process called Descriptive Programming, essentially hard coding the object path and properties necessary to identify and interact with an application object. There are very valid times when it's appropriate to leverage Descriptive Programming, the most common being when the object has dynamic attributes such as an incrementing ID (something dynamic yet predictable). I try not use Descriptive Programming unless it's absolutely necessary. I've seen two common approaches to Descriptive Programming that while clever, come at a high cost when maintenance becomes necessary. The first is using it for the entire automation framework. This approach will introduce major problems as soon as any aspect of the application has changed. Imagine having to go through thousands of lines of code trying to find every instance of descriptive programming for a common object that now needs to be updated. The second approach defines objects within the automation tool and then builds more objects based upon the first object. This is essentially reinventing the Object Repository concept and pointless in any tool containing object management capabilities. So how do bad practices like these get started? I'm aware of "Automation Experts" teaching "bad" practices like these. Be cautious where you're learning to use your automation tools. My suggestion is always get automation training from a reputable source.

Identification - To identify descriptive programming, look for object descriptions with properties such as class, name, etc. Remember that some implementation of descriptive programming is appropriate but if you see it across the entire automation framework, you're going to have trouble maintaining this automation in the future.

Also look for objects being created in source code based on descriptive programming concepts or pointing to Object Repository entries.

Resolution - Build a good Object Repository. Replace any excessive descriptive programming with Object Repository entries. It's going to be hard work but in the long run, will make maintaining the automation easier. Part of the question that needs asking is how did things get like this to begin with? If you have automation engineers building automation in this way, you need to change this practice. Enroll them in training and warn them about online sources that might be teaching practices like these.

Additionally - Object Recognition and management is one of the most critical aspects of Test Automation. Doing this well will be the difference in a successful vs. less successful automation effort.

10 - Unconventional Synchronization Strategy - I have a saying I share at QA Conferences, it goes like this... "Wait() might as well be called Hope() when it comes to test automation". An easy way to spot an entry level automation engineer is to look for the number of occurrence of the Wait() statement within their automation code. Wait() statements are the most common way inexperienced automation engineers use to allow time to pass before interacting more with the application via their test automation. Wait() is not a true synchronization strategy; it's a best guess at how long the automation engineer anticipates is necessary before executing additional test automation.

Most automation tools provide some way to determine if a screen is displayed, or if an object exists and is active. Be certain to understand how to detect these states of application objects and base the automation actions upon these state changes.

Identification - Look for Wait() statements, lots of Wait() statements. These are so common that you are likely to find hundreds of them in a poorly architected automation framework. Look for anything that does not actually monitor the state of the application but is involved in the timing of the automation code execution.

Resolution - Come up with a strong and consistent approach to synchronization. Anywhere that you find a Wait() statement, try to substitute with an approach of monitoring an object for state (exist or not exist). Let this approach drive the execution of the automation.

11 - Unconventional Data Strategy - Years ago I encountered an automation framework that was based upon spreadsheets referencing spreadsheets that in-turn referenced yet more spreadsheets. This was my first exposure to an overly abstract data-driven framework that was nearly impossible to maintain. Managing data in an automation framework can lead to some very obscure methodologies. On one hand, data lends itself to being organized in so many different ways. The best approach is to organize all the necessary data to fulfill a single test case into one single row of a datasheet. The next row will be for the next test case and so on. This makes for some long datasheets but they are actually quite easy to maintain.

Identification - Look for single spreadsheets designed to fulfill one test case. Similarly, look for one spreadsheet containing multiple tabs, one for each test case. Both of these approaches make it difficult to find and maintain test data for a large number of test cases.

Resolution - Plan your data strategy well. Start by going screen by screen in your application and document each field, drop-down, etc. into your datasheet. When you transition from one screen to the next, add a row with a pipe ("|") character in it to designate you have moved to the next screen. Consider setting aside the second row to indicate what screen these data fields pertain to. You can ignore this row when reading in the data. Use "camel case" (e.g. "UserName") and avoid using spaces when naming your data fields. Append Val (e.g. "ValTotalTax") in front of data fields that will be validated.

12 - Substitution of Functions for Reusable Actions - Understand the component structure of your automation tool. The automation tool set I work with leverages a concept called Reusable Actions. Remember as you build your framework, the test case data will drive the framework differently depending on the values within the datasheet. Each part of the framework should match-up to different functionality of the application under test. So a Point of Sale application would have automation components specifically designed to do a sale vs. a return. I try to have the automation components broken out in the same way as the application is broken out (e.g. One screen = One component). Unless your framework does not provide a component mechanism, do not use function libraries as a component tool as this seems to introduce over-abstraction into the automation framework.

Identification - Look for screen-by-screen functionality performed in function libraries. Also be aware of gigantic automation scripts that fulfill an entire test case in a single component. Both are common to encounter and both introduce problems in maintaining the automation framework.

Resolution - Build a flowchart to document the application flow. Create one component (Reusable action, etc.) for each segment of the flowchart. Provide conditional statements such as Case statements at each junction of the flowchart to analyze where to send the automation execution next. This approach makes the automation framework follow the application flow and will make it easier to maintain and enhance in the future.

13 - Reinvention of IDE Functionality - Two common areas I see reinvented within automation tool sets are the Object Repository and Register User Functions. It's important to understand the native way your tool set was intended to identify objects. Stick with this approach if at all possible, making it more likely that others can maintain it in the future. The same is true with built-in functionality. There should rarely be a reason to override native tool set functionality for your own take on how things should work. By doing this, you introduce greater confusion as to what a well-established function normally does, requiring specialized knowledge of your customization.

Identification - Be cautious what you find online, beware of anything over-complicates your approach. Look for RegisterUserFunc in your automation code and determine if this is overriding built-in functionality or adding new functionality. I typically find once a user starts to use these above methods, they propagate them throughout the automation framework.

Resolution - Revert back to any native object recognition best practices built into your tool set. Remove as much object interaction abstraction as possible to make troubleshooting and maintaining code easier in the future. Also evaluate any usage of RegisterUserFunc and ensure it's absolutely necessary. Revert to native IDE and tool set functionality whenever possible to ensure others can maintain the code going forward.

14 - Improper Usage of Subroutines and Functions - Having a good foundational understanding of the concepts of Function and Subroutines is important for any automation developer. Subroutines simply perform an action and pass nothing back to the calling code whereas a function can perform similar functionality and pass back return results to the calling code. I personally have been coding for over thirty years and am finding less and less need for subroutines and almost exclusively use functions. At the end of the day, you'll want to build code that not only fulfills the intended functionality but also enables easy maintenance for the next person who has to keep it running. With that said, I always return results from a function that can be helpful in maintaining the overall code. Subroutines simply don't have this capability and are used very infrequently in my code.

Identification - Identify subroutines across your automation effort and consider the type of information you might pass back to the calling routine if for no other purpose than to provide feedback as to the success or failure of the executed function. Change these subroutines over to functions and pass back useful troubleshooting details, which would aid in maintaining the automation in the future. Look for subroutines that use environment variables as a way of passing information back to calling routines. This bad practice is prevalent in many automation frameworks. Look for large functions that perform multiple tasks and consider if they can be broken into smaller, more simplified functions.

Resolution - Convert subroutines to functions that pass back useful information for troubleshooting and maintenance. Break large functions down into smaller, more maintainable functions. Be sure to talk with your automation team if you see them using subroutines and functions in unconventional ways.

15 - Not designed with Maintenance in Mind - Countless automation frameworks have been built without ever considering how they'll be maintained going forward. This can come from automation engineers focused on just getting something to work. QA management can also introduce this by not really understanding the realities and cost of having automation implemented within their testing organizations. Unfortunately, many automation tools are marketed with the idea that you simply click-and-record your way through the test suite. Consider a number of dry runs in maintaining your test automation. Have a more junior member of your team perform some basic maintenance and get the process hammered out before the test automation is in the critical path for application deployment.

Identification - Check with your senior test automation engineer regarding how they foresee future maintenance of the automation working. Typically one to two years after the original development is the time frame when this becomes most apparent. Most frameworks show their weaknesses after a release or two of the application they interact with. If you're identifying a lot of rework and major changes to the automation framework, then it's time to step back and evaluate if the framework should be continued or not.

Resolution - No questions asked, if your automation engineers have not had proper training, you will likely get less value from your framework than is possible. At this point, the challenge is, do you shore up the framework or start over? If you start over, make sure it's with an individual or team that has proper training.

16 - Inability to Scale - When building test automation, it's critical to consider how it will scale when run across multiple environments. It's easy to forget that once you've built the automation, you're likely to want it to run concurrently across more than one environment. For instance, can it run in different browser versions with the same results and performance? I've encountered automation frameworks that were tied to specific browser instances, users' machines, software builds and file systems. I refer to this as a "brittle framework" because of how easy it is to break the automation. It's critical to have an experienced automation engineer with the appropriate training, architect and build your automation framework.

Identification - Look for hard-coded paths, values, file names, user names, etc. within the automation framework. These are sure signs of a brittle framework. Look for dependencies on external files stored on the local file system or networked drives. Any change in these by the automation engineer or anyone else can break the test automation.

Resolution - Store all automation assets in a consistent approach. Include scripts, function libraries, datasheets, object repositories, etc. None of these items should need to be stored on the local file system if the automation framework is engineered correctly.

===== ROI Robbers =====

1 - Over-Abstraction

2 - "With" Statements

3 - Hard-Coded Data

4 - Environment Variables

5 - Code Duplication

6 - Undocumented Code

7 - Unconventional Looping Practices

8 - Unconventional Error Handling

9 - Unconventional Object Recognition

10 - Unconventional Synchronization Strategy

11 - Unconventional Data Strategy

12 - Substitution of Functions for Reusable Actions

13 - Reinvention of IDE Functionality

14 - Improper Use of Subroutines and Functions

15 - Not designed with Maintenance in Mind

16 - Inability to Scale

Glossary of Terms

Below you will find various terms used throughout this publication. Many are industry terms and others are ones I have created since my introduction to these tools.

Application Under Test (AUT): The application targeted for test automation.

Automated Quality Assurance: The act of verifying the quality of a software application by means of developed software that checks and validates aspects of that software.

Automated Test: A single test case that may have once been performed manually and can now be run using a test execution tool, or a test that was never practical to run manually but is a useful test run by a tool.

Automated Test Set: A group of tests with a primary common objective and secondary variations. For instance, testing the different tender types of a retail application. The primary objective would be Tender Type testing with the secondary variations being different tender types (e.g. Cash,

Check, Debit Card, Credit Card)

Automated Toolbox: The result of multiple iterations of automation development. The Automated Toolbox grows over time becoming more and more robust with the completion of each Automation Development Cycle.

Automation Candidate: An application or part of an application that is being considered for test automation development. Initially, Automation Candidates need to first go through an Automation Evaluation to understand how much if any of the candidate is a good fit for automation development.

Automation Development Cycle: The development of test automation in an iterative approach where a subsection of all the potential Good Automation Candidates are developed at a time. The Automation Development Cycle includes selecting the next Automated Workflow Candidate, the Automation Development, Training and adding to the Automated Toolbox.

Automation Evaluation: The process of ensuring the Application Under Test can reliably be interacted with using the automation tools and methodologies.

Automation Execution: Instantiating the completed test automation against the Application Under Test by executing the test through the automation or test management tool.

Automation Framework: A type of engine or approach to automating the Application Under Test. One of the better known frameworks within the HP tool-set is the usage of Business Process Testing Components which, when developed properly and strung together, can execute individual test cases. Custom Automation Frameworks are typically built using Reusable Actions that interpret data often fed in through a spreadsheet.

Automation Script: A entity of automation development that performs and validates actions against the Application Under Test. An automation script can refer to something as small as a single Business Process Testing component or a sequence of reusable actions strung together in a framework. This term is generally used to indicate that the test automation is performing the work, not a manual human tester.

Automation Test Strategy: A working term used to indicate the approach to be used in automating an Application Under Test. It may include whether to use Business Process Testing or to build a Custom Automation Framework for the automation aspects of the testing. It may also include how the application will logically be broken up such as functionally vs. physically.

Brittle Framework: The result of building test automation using poor or unconventional practices. Brittle test automation breaks with the most minor changes such as extra latency of the application under test. When encountering test automation that seems to break all the time, you likely have a brittle framework on your hands. Your first action should be to identify how and who engineered the test automation. Get your automation engineers the appropriate, training to ensure they are using the test automation tools as designed not as discovered.

Business Process Testing (BPT): A methodology developed by Hewlett Packard (HP) with the intent to allow earlier development of a test strategy. This methodology is best left to breaking up a test strategy into smaller segments, which can then be grouped together to construct an automated test. As a rule of thumb, no single Business Process Testing (BPT) Component should ever exceed a single screen. Additionally, there are times when a single complex screen should be broken into separate components but for the best organization and manageability of these BPT Components, keep them to a single screen. It may be interesting to note that a common mistake when using the BPT methodology is to have a single component exercise an entire test case. This approach will lead to significant redundant code and will impact maintainability in the long run.

Click-and-Record: A method often used to sell automation software to customers new to test automation. The process usually follows the clicking of a Record button within the test automation software and then the test case being manually performed, thus allowing the test automation tool to capture the steps and object properties being interacted with. These tests can sometimes be run a number of times after the initial Click-and-Record session but rarely execute reliably for any useful length of time due to dynamic nature of most computing environments and other factors.

Descriptive Programming: An object recognition approach that bypasses the usage of the Object Repository and directly includes the properties of an object within the automation code. This approach eliminates the need for an object repository but can be problematic if objects within the application change, as they may no longer be identified by the automation code unless all the instances referencing that object are updated throughout the code.

Evaluation Test: A single, individual test within the Automation Evaluation typically used to verify one aspect of the Application Under Test.

Hewlett Packard (HP): A vendor of test automation tools including QuickTest Pro (QTP), Unified Functional Testing (UFT), Lean Functional Testing (LeanFT), Quality Center (QC) and Application Life-cycle Management (ALM).

IDE: Integrated Development Environment

Manual Tester: A human being performing testing by interacting directly with the Application Under Test, and typically not using any aspect of automation in their testing efforts.

Object Repository: A test automation asset that centrally stores properties to identify objects within the Application Under Test.

Reusable Action: A term used within the Hewlett Packard tool-set to indicate a section of functionality that will likely be joined to another Reusable Action to implement additional test functionality. Reusable actions are typically used in building Custom Automation Frameworks. Reusable Actions can conditionally call other Reusable Actions programmatically, which makes them very flexible for frameworks that need to perform differently depending upon the strategy used to direct the test.

ROI: Return on Investment

ROI Robbers: Implementation of a tool, concept or approach that has an impact on typical and potential return on investment (ROI) within given technology, framework or methodology.

Run Off the Tracks: The result of test automation encountering a situation not expected and therefore stopping before the test has run to completion. I prefer to let my test automation "Run Off the Tracks" instead of building in excessive error handling. This approach allows the automation engineer to focus on core functionality and brings awareness to areas of the automation that need updating.

Test Asset: A general term that could refer to an automated test component, documentation related to testing or any individual entity that is part of the testing effort.

Test Automation: The usage of a software tool set to perform tasks typically completed manually by a human being which is now automated by a computer.

Test Automation Development Engineer: An individual with both Software Development experience as well as Quality Assurance experience.

The Automation Miracle: The mythical realm where test automation manifests through simple Click-and-Record sessions resulting in endless test cases that run forevermore. The Automation Miracle is typically inclusive of every environment including Windows and Mobile, IE, Firefox and Chrome, where one automation script works across all environments seamlessly. The Automation Miracle typically comes up with vendors selling test automation and users who have bought test automation software but never tried to implement it. It's worth noting here because while the term "Automation Miracle" will not be used, the concept of what automation can provide to an organization will be encountered when exploring the world of test automation.

Test Automation Reality Check: A regularly scheduled event where the following two items are evaluated with the automation development activities.

1) **QA Process**: Does the test automation have the necessary validations built into it to fulfill the job of Automated Quality Assurance?

2) **Maintainable/Sustainable Development**: Does the test automation utilize known best practices to enable the developed solution to be maintained by most software engineers with minimal ramp-up experience?

Tune the Object Repository: The technique of narrowing down just the properties that are necessary for an Object Repository to reliably interact with the Application Under Test.

Acknowledgments

Like most things in life, we rarely end up where we are based solely upon our own efforts.

Family, friends, colleagues and others have had a significant impact in my life. I wanted to take a few moments to acknowledge some of those that have really been influential in the helping me to grow into the person I've become.

I'd like to start by thanking my Mother, Peggy and Father, Marvin Paskal for investing so much in the possibilities of my life. They continually encouraged and supported me as I was growing up, making many possibilities a reality for me. Although I greatly struggled through school, they realized I had a different way of learning and understanding things, from a very different perspective than most. Mom and Dad went out of their way to provide the types of tools an experimenter like myself needed to analyze and understand the world. From my first electronics kit and soldering iron to my first computer, a Commodore Vic 20, they allowed me the chance to explore the world through the imagination of a tinkerer, experimenter and tester. Without your willingness to take a chance on these investments in my life, I am certain things would have turned out very differently.

I'd like to thank Eddie Shultz, a friend of my Father's and an incredible design engineer. Eddie took me under his wing at an early age and mentored me in the basics of electronics and design. He modeled for me, how powerful the investment of one-person's life into another can really be. I think of your example often Eddie as I now get the chance to pour into the lives of others.

I want to thank my Director, Ed Lucas, who had the wisdom and foresight to realize that with good tools should come good training. Thank you Ed for sending us to training to learn how to use our tools as designed, not discovered. I'm certain that while this decision came at an extra cost, it produced an exponential return on that training investment. That training is still in good use today.

I'd like to recognize Joe Colantonio, my friend and fellow automation guru who, like myself, loves to share his passion for test automation with others. Joe, your dedication to learning and sharing your knowledge to so many of us through your Test Talks podcast and JoeColantonio.com is invaluable.

To my good friend Keith Brooks, who took a chance on me many years ago and brought me into a formal QA role. Thanks Keith for the opportunities to learn and experiment with some great test automation tools. Thank you for being such a good friend and supporter of my whole family and myself.

Two people that must get recognized are my good friends Mark Bentsen and Jeff Kemper. Some of the smartest and most supportive men I know. I have learned countless lessons from you both and am grateful to call you brothers and friends. Thank you Mark for making opportunities for me to stretch my automation skills in new and exciting ways as we blaze new trails in test innovation. Thank you Jeff for your technical genius and willingness to share the exciting roads you have discovered as a fellow automation innovator. Guys, "let us consider how we may spur one another on toward love and good deeds" - Hebrews 10:24

Lastly, continuing thanks and blessing to my Bride of 28 years. Cindy, your support and encouragement over these wonderful years are invaluable. You encourage me to be the creative Man God has set me out to be. I love you more than words can describe.

* * *

Printed in Great Britain
by Amazon